Sparkling Harvest

The Seasons of the Vine

Sparkling

HARRY N. ABRAMS, INC., PUBLISHERS

Harvest

The Seasons of the Vine

Introduction by **Hugh Johnson**

"Napa Wines" by **Robert Louis Stevenson**

Text by **Jamie and Jack Davies**

Photographs by **James Alinder**

Editor: Adele Westbrook
Designer: Lorraine Ferguson

Library of Congress Cataloging-in-Publication Data

Davies, Jamie, date.
    Sparkling harvest : the seasons of the vine / introduction by
Hugh Johnson ; "Napa wines" by Robert Louis Stevenson ;
text by Jamie and Jack Davies ; photographs by James Alinder.
       p.   cm.
    Includes index.
    ISBN 0–8109–1247–3 (clothbound)
    1. Schramsberg Vineyards and Winery—History. 2. Sparkling
wines—California—Calistoga. I. Davies, Jack, date. II. Title.
TP557.D385 1997
641.2'2'0979419—DC21   96–50166

endpaper map:
Courtesy of the Napa County Department of Public Works

above:
Spring Storm Clearing

pages 2–3:
Ripe Chardonnay Grapes

Published in 1997 by Harry N. Abrams, Incorporated, New York
All rights reserved. No part of the contents of this book may be
reproduced without the written permission of the publisher
Printed and bound in Japan

Harry N. Abrams, Inc.
100 Fifth Avenue
New York, N.Y. 10011
www.abramsbooks.com

Contents

Foreword

As we find ourselves celebrating more than thirty years at Schramsberg, in the Napa Valley, we rejoice in the memorable and elegant history in which it has been our good fortune to share.

One of the more remarkable moments in that history was when Robert Louis Stevenson visited the Valley on his honeymoon in 1880, and spent considerable time at Schramsberg. Later, back in Scotland, he wrote the wonderful book *Silverado Squatters* in which he dramatically described the evolving wine industry he had discovered.

"The beginning of a wine planting is like the beginning of mining for the precious metals; the wine-grower also 'prospects.' One corner of the land after another is tried with one kind of grape after another. This is a failure; that is better; a third best. So, bit by bit, they grope about for their Clos Vougeot and Lafite. Those lodes and pockets of earth, more precious than the precious ores, that yield inimitable fragrance and soft fire; whose virtuous Bonanzas, where the soil has sublimated under sun and stars to something finer, and the wine is bottled poetry . . ."

Our enthusiasm and love for wine making flows not only from the relationship it affords to nature, but also from the pleasure of continually learning and discovering what it provides. One has to be grateful for that opportunity. We also know that the unusual fraternity of good will that exists in this world of wine is another "virtuous Bonanza."

We thank Jim Alinder greatly for his collaboration in this work. His artistry with the camera and his gentle, patient understanding are treasures. Also great thanks and appreciation to our dear friend Hugh Johnson, who has been so kind as to prepare the gracious Introduction to this work.

It is impossible to acknowledge all of the people who have helped us at some point along the way. A number are mentioned in the text, but the list is far from complete. Certainly we are indebted to André and Dimitri Tchelistcheff, who carefully guided and trained us in the beginning. And we cannot fail to mention some of our own co-workers who have been involved in wine making with us for years and years. Our winemakers over time: Harold Osborne, Greg Fowler, Alan Tenscher, and Mike Reynolds. The ever-ready hands from Mexico without whose help, over these decades, we would never have made it: Jaime Aguirre, Ramon Vierra, Jorge Ceja-Valdez, Efren Torres— to mention only a few who have been on the path the longest; each of them over twenty years.

Worker's Still Life

clockwise from top left:
The Dining Room
The Kitchen
Ready for Christmas
Decorations on Dining Room Wall
Hugh's Room

And to Beth Wagner who showed up one day as a temporary secretary and never left. Then, of course, there is the new joy of having two of our sons, Bill and Hugh, working closely with us.

And finally, to our small band of loyal partners who have supported us steadily and never looked back.

We hope these words and pictures will adequately express our appreciation for our good fortune and the wonderful world that surrounds all of us.

Jamie and Jack Davies
Schramsberg Vineyards, Napa Valley

Introduction

Schramsberg. It's part of the language now. The name has the authoritative ring of a classic. Bollinger, Roederer, Krug—why do Germans make such wonderful bubbly?

Jack and Jamie Davies aren't in the least German. But they took up where Jacob Schram left off; Schram the pioneer who found a California heaven—and was found in it by Robert Louis Stevenson.

And I, in my wilder fantasies, am the R.L.S. who found Jack and Jamie. Not the poet, nor the romancer, but at least a writer who climbed through the winding woods to the clearing where Schram's old white house stands in all its unreality.

It was my first visit to the Napa Valley and the Davieses had been at Schramsberg just one year. Nothing had prepared me (nor them either, I suspect) for the impact of this country outside time. It was the tense stillness of the forest, above all, that gripped me. Its trails, winding out of sight to lonely dwellings among redwood and mesquite and maple, suggested a remote age, a lost civilization—which was not far from the truth.

But the first flowering of this golden land was cut short by Prohibition, and the effects of Prohibition lasted three times as long as the amendment itself.

Hence Schramsberg's long sleep, its cool rock tunnels empty and the paint peeling from its wide veranda, while America went without the benison it could bring.

How was the Napa Valley in those days? Not deserted, but worked more in faith and hope than for profit. André Tchelistcheff at Beaulieu was the high priest; Joe Heitz his precocious pupil. To the half-dozen long-established larger wineries still soldiering patiently on you could add the visionary names of Stony Hill, Souverain, Mayacamas—and momentously, that very year, the new Robert Mondavi winery.

With Mondavi the valley perceptibly changed gear. But it would be a few years before many people knew what was brewing at Schramsberg. Sparkling wines are long in gestation, and of all wines need the most patient attention to every detail. The Davieses had to learn everything the hard way, applying to the very different conditions of California the lessons they learned from the creators of champagne.

All credit to the Champenois that they saw Schramsberg as an ally, the Napa Valley as their challenge too. The spirit of wine that Jack frequently invokes drew these distant Frenchmen into a natural partnership. And when they tasted the early

"The Riddler's Night Out"

successes of Schramsberg, they knew that they had to come to Napa, too.

What are the special qualities in Napa grapes that Schramsberg was able to reveal? (For the vineyards provide the flavors; champagne is not made in Bordeaux.) They are not, after all, the rich resonant flavors that Napa famously gives to its Cabernet and Chardonnay. For sparkling wines liveliness is all; not just in the bubbles but in the flavors and aromas that cross your palate. Liveliness, and creamy texture.

As Dom Pérignon discovered, a blend can be greater than the sum of its parts. The Davies triumph was to reinterpret the classic champagne blend using grapes that ripen far earlier; are picked in late summer, in fact, rather than in the chill of autumn.

And then there are Jacob Schram's cool dark tunnels in the rock; the Napa equivalent of Champagne's ancient chalk quarries, essential for the slow maturing of the wine on the yeast.

But as with everything connected with great wines, the more you analyze it the less you can pinpoint the magic. First it is the vineyard, then it is the grapes, then the cellars—all true. But finally it is the palate and its accumulated judgment.

I salute a great judge who has persevered to give the world a unique, yet happily repeatable, pleasure.

— *Hugh Johnson*

from left:
Ripe Grapes in Flute
An 1880s Barrel Hoop—Still Around

The Centuries-old Redwood Circle

Ferns and Moss in the Winter

"Napa Wines" from *Silverado Squatters*, 1880

I was interested in California wine. Indeed, I am interested in all wines and have been all my life, from the raisin wine that a school-fellow kept secreted in his play-box up to my last discovery, those notable Valtellines that shone upon the board of Caesar.

Some of us, kind old Pagans, watch with dread the shadows falling on the age: how the unconquerable worm invades the sunny terraces of France, and the Bordeaux is no more, and the Rhone a mere Arabia Petraea. Chateau Neuf is

Pinot Noir Turning Color

dead, and I have never tasted it; Hermitage—
a hermitage indeed from all life's sorrows—lies
expiring by the river. And in the place of these
imperial elixirs, beautiful to every sense, gem-hued,
flower-scented, dream-compellers:—behold upon
the quays at Cette the chemicals arrayed; behold the
analyst at Marseilles, raising hands in obsecration,
attesting god Lyoeus, and the vats staved in, and
the dishonest wines poured forth among the sea.
It is not Pan only; Bacchus, too, is dead.

 If wine is to withdraw its most poetic coun-
tenance, the sun of the white dinner-cloth, a deity
to be invoked by two or three, all fervent, hushing
their talk, degusting tenderly, and storing reminis-
cences—for a bottle of good wine, like a good act,
shines ever in the retrospect—if wine is to desert us,
go thy ways, old Jack! Now we begin to have com-
punctions, and look back at the brave bottles squan-
dered upon dinner-parties, where the guests drank
grossly, discussing politics the while, and even the
schoolboy "took his whack," like licorice water.
And at the same, we look timidly forward, with a
spark of hope, to where the new lands, already
weary of producing gold, begin to green with vineyards. A nice point in human history falls to be
decided by Californian and Australian wines.

 Wine in California is still in the experimen-
tal stage; and when you taste a vintage, grave
economical questions are involved. The beginning
of a wine planting is like the beginning of mining
for the precious metals: the wine-grower also
"prospects." One corner of the land after another is
tried with one kind of grape after another. This
is a failure; that is better; a third best. So, bit by bit,
they grope about for their Clos Vougeot and Lafite.
Those lodes and pockets of earth, more precious
than the precious ores, that yield inimitable
fragrance and soft fire; whose virtuous Bonanzas,
where the soil has sublimated under sun and stars
to something finer, and the wine is bottled poetry:
these still lie undiscovered; chaparral conceals,
thicket embowers them; the miner chips the rock
and wanders farther, and the grizzly muses undis-
turbed. But there they bide their hour, awaiting
their Columbus; and nature nurses and prepares
them. The smack of Californian earth shall linger
on the palate of your grandson.

 Meanwhile the wine is merely a good wine;
the best that I have tasted better than a Beaujolais,
and not unlike. But the trade is poor; it lives from
hand to mouth, putting its all into experiments,
and forced to sell its vintages. To find one properly
matured, and bearing its own name, is to be
fortune's favorite.

opposite:
Vineyard Meets the Forest

Jacob Schram

Bearing its own name, I say, and dwell upon the innuendo.

"You want to know why California wine is not drunk in the States?" a San Francisco wine merchant said to me, after he had shown me through his premises. "Well, here's the reason."

And opening a large cupboard, fitted with many small drawers, he proceeded to shower me all over with a great variety of gorgeously tinted labels, blue, red, or yellow, stamped with crown or coronet, and hailing from such a profusion of *clos* and *chateaux,* that a single department could scarce have furnished forth the names. But it was strange that all looked unfamiliar.

"Chateau X_____?" said I. "I never heard of that."

"I dare say not," said he. "I had been reading one of X_____'s novels."

They were all castles in Spain! But that sure enough is the reason why California wine is not drunk in the States.

Napa Valley has long been a seat of the wine-growing industry. It did not begin here, as it does too often, in the low valley lands along the river, but took at once to the rough foot-hills, where alone it can expect to prosper. A basking inclination, and stones, to be a reservoir of the day's heat, seem necessary to the soil for wine; the grossness of the earth must be evaporated, its marrow daily melted and refined for ages; until at length these clods that break below our footing, and to the eye appear but common earth, are truly and to the perceiving mind, a masterpiece of nature. The dust of Richebourg, which the wind carries away, what an apotheosis of the dust! Not man himself can seem a stranger child of that brown, friable powder, than the blood and sun in that old flask behind the faggots.

A Californian vineyard, one of man's outposts in the wilderness, has features of its own. There is nothing here to remind you of the Rhine or Rhone, of the low *cote d'or,* or the infamous and scabby deserts of Champagne; but all is green, solitary, covert. We visited two of them, Mr. Schram's and Mr. M'Eckron's, sharing the same glen.

Some way down the valley below Calistoga, we turned sharply to the south and plunged into the thick of the wood. A rude trail rapidly mounting; a little stream tinkling by on the one hand, big

Schram's Old Stone Wall

enough perhaps after the rains, but already yielding up its life; overhead and on all sides a bower of green and tangled thicket, still fragrant and still flower-bespangled by the early season, where thimble-berry played the part of our English hawthorn, and the buckeyes were putting forth their twisted horns of blossom: through all this, we struggled toughly upwards, canted to and fro by the roughness of the trail, and continually switched across the face by sprays of leaf or blossom. This last is no great inconvenience at home; but here in California it is a matter of some moment. For in all woods and by every wayside there prospers an abominable shrub or weed, called poison oak, whose very neighbourhood is venomous to some, and whose actual touch is avoided by the most impervious.

The two houses, with their vineyards, stood each in a green niche of its own in this steep and narrow forest dell. Though they were so near, there was already a good difference in level; and Mr. M'Eckron's head must be a long way under the feet of Mr. Schram. No more had been cleared than was

from left:
Old Winery at M'Eckron's

The Winter Brings Waterfalls

from top:
The Schram House
Jacob and Annie Schram with Family and Friends
Schram Aging Cask

necessary for cultivation; close around each oasis ran the tangled wood; the glen enfolds them; there they lie basking in sun and silence, concealed from all but the clouds and mountain birds.

Mr. M'Eckron's is a bachelor establishment; a little bit of a wooden house, a small cellar hard by in the hillside, and a patch of vines planted and tended single-handed by himself. He had but recently begun; his vines were young, his business young also; but I thought he had the look of the man who succeeds. He hailed from Greenock: he remembered his father putting him into Mons Meg, and that touched me home; and we exchanged a word or two of Scotch, which pleased me more than you would fancy.

Mr. Schram's, on the other hand, is the oldest vineyard in the valley, eighteen years old, I think; yet he began a penniless barber, and even after he had broken ground up here with his black malvoisies, continued for long to tramp the valley with his razor. Now, his place is the picture of prosperity; stuffed birds in the veranda, cellars far dug into the hillside, and resting on pillars like a bandit's cave: all trimness, varnish, flowers, and sunshine, among the tangled wildwood. Stout, smiling Mrs. Schram, who had been to Europe and apparently all about the States for pleasure, enter-

tained Fanny in the veranda, while I was tasting wines in the cellar. To Mr. Schram this was a solemn office; his serious gusto warmed my heart; prosperity had not yet wholly banished a certain neophite and girlish trepidation, and he followed every sip and read my face with proud anxiety. I tasted all. I tasted every variety and shade of Schramberger, red and white Schramberger, Burgundy Schramberger, Schramberger Hock, Schramberger Golden Chasselas, the latter with a

notable bouquet, and I fear to think how many more. Much of it goes to London—most, I think; and Mr. Schram has a great notion of the English taste.

In this wild spot, I did not feel the sacred-ness of ancient cultivation. It was still raw, it was no Marathon, and no Johannisberg; yet the stirring sunlight, and the growing vines, and the vats and bottles in the cavern, made a pleasant music for the mind. Here, also, earth's cream was being skimmed

Olive Tree, Shadows, and Vineyard

and garnered; and the London customers can taste, such as it is, the tang of the earth in this green valley. So local, so quintessential is a wine, that it seems the very birds in the veranda might communicate a flavour, and that romantic cellar influence the bottle next to be uncorked in Pimlico, and the smile of jolly Mr. Schram might mantle in the glass.

But these are but experiments. All things in this new land are moving farther on: the wine-vats and the miner's blasting tools but picket for a night, like Bedouin pavilions; and tomorrow, to fresh woods! This stir of change and these perpetual echoes of the moving footfall, haunt the land. Men move eternally, still chasing Fortune; and, fortune found, still wander. As we drove back to Calistoga the road lay empty of mere passengers, but its green side was dotted with the camps of travelling families: one cumbered with a great waggonful of household stuff, settlers going to occupy a ranche they had taken up in Mendocino, or perhaps Tehama County; another, a party in dust-coats, men and women, whom we found camped in a grove on the roadside, all on pleasure bent, with a Chinaman to cook for them, and who waved their hands to us as we drove by.

— *Robert Louis Stevenson*

from left:
Schram's Iron Gate
Schram's Cook, Ming Sing Li

The Seasons of the Vine

Seasons of Beginning

Jamie and I followed along behind Joe Torres. We could hear the softly falling drizzle. We could hear our feet on the damp wild vetch and mustard. Our path was along the western slopes of the Napa Valley, high on the Mayacamas Range.

The year was 1965. We had just purchased a pioneer wine estate gone fallow since Prohibition. Nothing had happened here on the Schramsberg estate for years. And we had never lived on—or made a living from—the land.

Joe Torres was foreman of the pristine Draper Vineyards on a neighboring mountainside. A new friend, Jerome Draper, had said, "Ask Joe to look it over for you. He'll tell you what you're up against."

Having already closed the escrow we were perhaps a little late in finding out what we were up against, but here we were walking with Joe in the rain; beginning to learn.

He didn't say much for awhile. Just led us along the sloping land, looking quietly at the dead vines, the robust poison oak, the dainty, new fir trees. He knelt down and picked up a handful of soil, considered it and cast it away. Then he walked on under the overcast sky. How quiet and remote this place seemed.

Schram's Old Vines—Still Alive in the Forest

The Roadside Creek in Winter

opposite:

Madrone Tree

As we headed back down the hill Joe backed us up against a tree and said, "You're going to talk to a lot of people. You're going to talk to the farm advisor, and he'll tell you what he thinks. You'll talk to the boys at the tractor shop and hear what they have to say. Mr. Draper will give you his ideas. So will I. You'll hear plenty, and the advice will mostly be different. One day you must make up your own minds how to go ahead.

"But believe this, if nothing else. Don't start second-guessing yourselves. Stick to what you believe and you'll be O.K."

We had been touched by the spirit for the first time—but not the last.

*I*t was an earlier beginning—1842. The young man was sixteen years old. His name was Jacob Schram. He had been born in the Rhineland, in the town of Pfeddersheim. He was getting off the boat on Staten Island, an immigrant to America.

He could not have known what lay ahead. Learning to be a barber, sailing across the Caribbean, crossing the Panama Isthmus, arriving in San Francisco and opening a barber shop. He later moved to the Napa Valley; continuing his barbering. Remembering his roots in the vinelands of Germany and likely wanting to be part of an emerging effort, in 1862, he purchased a very large piece of mountainland on the western slopes of the Valley.

It was a dramatic time in many ways. The Civil War had just started. Count Agoston Haraszthy had just completed his historic trip to Europe and returned with cuttings of hundreds of wine grape varieties. Schram was thirty-six years old.

He started clearing the virgin land. He built a small cabin to serve as his home. He brought in Chinese workers to help him dig underground wine caves. He remained a barber to provide income, and talked with everyone he could about how to make wine.

Map of Schramsberg, June 1885

pages 34–35:
The Original Nineteenth-Century Cabin for Chinese Workers

Schramsberg Vineyard
JACOB SCHRAM, PROPRIETOR.

St. Helena,
Napa Co. Cal.
U.S.A.

St. Helena, June 1st 1895

A. Aalbern,
Excelsior Spgs, Clay Co., Mo

Dear Sir:— I have taken the liberty to enclose a price-list of our wines, and would ask your perusal of the same. As you are already familiar with our brands, it is unnecessary for me to refer to their quality. Having on hand a large stock of fine old wines, made of the best varieties of French and German grapes, which I wish to dispose of, would be pleased to receive a renewal of your patronage.

Thanking you for past favors and

Letter from Jacob Schram, June 1895

He did well. His wines made their way coast to coast and even to Europe. We have a charming handwritten note from Jacob to a gentleman in Clay County, Missouri which reads:

"As you are already familiar with our brand it is unnecessary for me to refer to their quality. Having on hand a stock of fine old wines made of the best varieties of French and German grapes—I would be pleased to receive a renewal of your patronage."

He had to be a salesman too.

In 1880, when Robert Louis Stevenson came to
the Valley with his new bride, they moved into the
abandoned mining town of Silverado, on Mount St.
Helena near Schram's vineyard. He visited Schram
and later wrote extensively about Schramsberg.
Imagine being there, through Stevenson's eyes.

> "His place is the picture of prosperity;
> stuffed birds in the veranda, cellars far dug
> into the hillside, and resting on pillars like
> a bandit's cave: all trimness, varnish, flowers,
> and sunshine, among the tangled wildwood
> . . . the stirring sunlight, and the growing
> vines, and the vats and bottles in the cavern,
> made a pleasant music for the mind."

Schram died in 1905 at the age of 79.
A new season began.

Spring Blooms

Between a succession of new owners, the thirteen-year assault of Prohibition, the Depression, and World War II Schramsberg went into a long decline. Douglas Pringle acquired the property in 1951 and made a serious effort to restore it, but without success.

The stage was now set for our season.

On the first day we saw Schramsberg no one lived there. The dirt road up from the highway wandered through redwoods and fir emerging at the clearing where Jacob's first cabin had stood. In front of us was a cave, opening into the hill alongside the old winery building. A California Historical Landmark plaque caught our eye. To our right was the old barn, with its attractive cornerstone—built in 1884 —and to the left, the grand Victorian home the Schrams had built in 1889. Further over, the huge underground cellars and, high above us, the abandoned vineyards. We walked in the silence. It was like a frozen cameo, but inspiring. We looked at each other. We had to try this!

from top:
The Victorian Veranda
The Original Barn, 1884
Historical Landmark Plaque

The Road In

Seasons of Farming

The grapevine may be one of our few companions that is as old as our oldest ancestor. Think about it. The first vine appeared somewhere around the Black Sea—we don't know exactly where or when. Men and women carried the vine with them in every direction, and tried to induce it to live wherever they found themselves. In many places it has taken root enthusiastically.

People have learned to succeed with the vine by asking questions such as: "What makes it grow best?" "How should we plant and transplant it?" We also ask about spacing. If we plant vines close together, do we force them to struggle for nourishment—pushing their roots deeper, and gaining more character from the soil? Or must we plant the vines further apart, let them share the nourishment in a more balanced way, and provide more sun and air to the leaves? Which way is best?

And there is the sun. Sometimes the vine gets just the right amount of sun—sometimes too much. Since there is nothing we can do about the sun, we must learn how to best train the vine. Do we develop more leaf canopy? How? And which slope of the hill creates the most cooling air movement?

We faced the task of replanting the abandoned vineyards. Where to start? How?

Pinot Noir in August

We had lots of help. An old friend, Ben Huber, rented surveyor's instruments, then came over and helped us lay out the vine rows. Joe Torres kept reappearing. One day he sat us down under a tree and handed us some heavy twigs, some sharp knives, and said "You've got to learn how to bud—practice on these willow branches so you won't ruin the vines."

When it came time to actually put the rootstock in the ground, we had gone to a nursery and purchased the first vines. They come tied in bundles of fifty rootstocks and one needs to store them until ready to plant. That storage is usually accomplished by burying the bundles in a sand pile until they're needed.

Just at that time a new notion was emerging. "Store the rootstock in the sand upside down so the energy is running opposite gravity until you actually plant them." We tried that new idea and stored our rootstock upside down in the sand. Then we began planting day by day. Later we were astonished when we heard a rumor sweeping through the Valley—"those crazy city folks don't know what they're doing. They're planting their rootstock upside down in their vineyard!" It took us months to dispel that myth.

Rain is a crucial factor. In our fifth year of trying to be grape cultivators it rained for over fourteen days straight. Our newly replanted vineyard had not yet established the vigorous ground cover of grass that holds down the tilled soil. And the rains kept coming. A ditch began to appear right down the middle of the vineyard. We tried, in the pouring rain, to create diversions with sand bags and trenches. Futile. The ditch gradually grew deeper. More quickly than we could believe, we had a gully waist deep! We lost twenty-five or thirty vines that had to be replanted, which meant three extra years of waiting for their first grapes.

Of course, on the other hand, it may not rain. A little drought we think is O. K. It stresses the vine we say. Makes for intense flavor and aroma. But what if the stress is so severe that it kills? To prevent that we irrigate. Drip irrigation was invented in Israel for orchards and had been adapted around the world for other uses. We were among the first to try it in California vineyards. We didn't want too much irrigation, but we didn't want to lose our young vines either. We learned to lay out the lines, find the right dripper, and ration the water. All went well until the coyotes decided they had found a new source of water and chewed into the hoses.

Stacked Grape Stakes

Forest in Winter Rain

Sleeping in Winter—Ready for Pruning

pages 48–49:
The Vines Move Along

*Grape Vines
and Mustard*

Hard At It!

Picking at Dawn

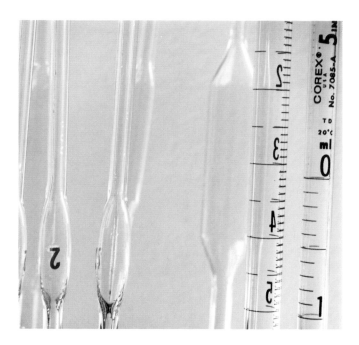

In the fall the vines shed their leaves and become dormant. It's an important time: they recover and prepare for the next season. We need to prune them back carefully to arrange the set as best we can. We shifted from one pattern to another over the years as we adapted, with the vine, to the patterns of earth, sun, and rain.

As the winter rains come to an end, the weather warms. The tiny buds on each cane begin to swell and finally burst, and the first leaves appear.

You walk the rows, examining each vine and deciding how to help it. A most satisfying task. Nonproductive canes must be removed. The plant must be secured on the stake against high winds. You stop and look back down the row. It's very clear to the eye: neatness and readiness. You know you have accomplished something. You almost feel the vines saying "thank you, well done."

It's this time of year—the spring—when you feel your partnership with the vine most intensely. You have been doing your best and the vine is responding.

Now frost threatens. On our mountainside the marine air currents help greatly. If we have laid out the vineyard correctly, the breeze should suffice. But in the valley below, the growers face night after night of war. Wind machines, orchard heaters,

Lifting Grape Clusters into Wine Press

or protecting water spray are the weapons. Our friend Jim Nichelini got up seventeen nights one year to protect the vines by spraying. He ran out of water and lost the whole crop on night eighteen.

April gives way to May, then June arrives. Tiny berries (at first they look like green buckshot) slowly swell and push out. Bunches fill in. Finally, in early July the first traces of color appear on the Pinot Noir. We pass through the rows again and again—not only in our own vineyards but in all those from whom we purchase fruit. Carefully selected individual grapes are picked to provide a true sample of what is out there—and tell us what is to come.

The sun shimmers hot in the sky. Good thing you have on a big hat as you move at an angle across the field. You want to select single berries from random bunches all across the major expanse of vineyard. Single berries. First from the vine on your right: reach in, high up, out of sight, so as not to prejudice the sample by picking only the grapes easily seen and reached. Alternate: a grape from the top of a bunch next. Now from a vine on your left, take a grape from a bunch on the outside; don't choose it—just reach out and pick at random.

Push the canes carefully out of the way and crawl on your knees under the wires and across into

Checking Grapes for Harvest

the next row. Keep moving along that row, then crawl over to the next, and so gradually work your way across the field. The sun blazes. Pick one hundred berries at random, get in the truck, and drive back to the winery.

In the coolness of the Laboratory, juice is pressed from the samples and examined. How much sugar has Nature created at this point? How much acid is present? Is there any sign of mildew or bunch rot? Is it a true sample?

At last the harvest is at hand. We hope it doesn't rain. The trucks and equipment must not fail. Boxes and knives must be ready. The crew needs water bottles and Porta-potties. Harvest is like an opening night, but there will be only one performance. On the day the grapes are right we must have them. Not two days later. Not two days earlier.

Imagine what it is like to be ready to hand pick forty tons of grapes in one day and find that you need to pick eighty tons instead, because the sampling was not accurate and some grapes are riper than you had thought.

Where will the extra pickers come from? We don't have the necessary boxes or trucks. Once in awhile this scenario plays itself out negatively and Nature scores an unfortunate blow on us.

But when our sampling and timing are right, and the gondola moves away behind the tractor, the pickers sing as they work. One may run full tilt with his box balanced on his head: reaching the vehicle just as it gathers speed, flinging his load onto the grapes already there. "Cinco!" He shouts out his number, and the foreman credits his addition to the treasure. You sense competition. No, maybe a ritual. Certainly a performance.

It's grand slam time. Red grapes, green grapes. Up at first light. Fog all around, chill in the air. Hands warming by a small fire. Straining tractors, snorting trucks. Color. Energy. Spirit.

We think back to a conversation with a Farm Advisor a season or two back. We had been walking through our upper vineyards, which were being replanted a year or so later than the first section below. He looked skeptically about. "I really don't see how you can expect to do anything here. It's too steep. The soil isn't much."

But here we were in the harvest—as it has been for centuries beyond memory. And we think again of Stevenson's words: "We look timidly forward, with a spark of hope, to where the new lands, already weary of producing gold, begin to green with vineyards."

Picker Loads Gondola

Seasons of Learning

The village of Hautvilliers is on the chalky mountains of Champagne above the river Marne in France. A very old place.

In the late 1600s, Dom Pérignon, a Benedictine monk, made wine here. Although no one makes wine there today, the estate is lovingly cared for by the present owners, Moët-Chandon. And the presence of Dom Pérignon's spirit is unmistakable. Walking in Hautvilliers, we sensed that he had been trying to do what we are trying to do. His tools were not the same as ours, but his goal was. His methods were not identical to ours, but his ideas were similar.

Sparkling wines were actually not developed first in France. They emerged in Italy and England around 1660-1670.

But Dom Pérignon worked with artistry and dedication to help improve the brilliant sparkling wines we may enjoy today. He worked at making white wine from red grapes. And he perfected many techniques for making consistent and reliable sparkling wine. But of his many contributions to the art, the most significant and personal was the blending of several wines harmoniously to form the base wine.

This was a great moment in the culture of the world. And Dom Pérignon felt it. The lore tells

Champagne and Sunflowers

pages 64–65:
Two Miles of Caves—Three Million Bottles

us that, gazing at one of his first sparkling bottles, he said "There are stars in the wine!" His first champagne—and the spirit—was born.

Edmund Maudiere, our friend and now retired winemaker at Moët-Chandon, guided us on our walk through the world of Dom Pérignon. Edmund is one of the great citizens of Champagne. He is rarely satisfied, but always patient.

He cocks his head when he says something like "Well, we really don't know. We have to try that. We have to let the wines age for a few years and see what happens. We are not going to let our quality escape us." He talks like this about new techniques for clearing bottles. And he talks like this about new practices in the vineyards.

New? Yes—he's still refining his craft, building on over 350 years of cumulative experience.

Once, early in our efforts, Edmund visited us in the Napa Valley. Watching the way we were stacking our bottles for aging, he said, "Why don't you stack them on themselves instead of separating them with the wooden lath? Use the cave walls to support them? You'll save a lot of space while the wine ages. I think it will work." We followed his advice and it did work. He also talked with us about yeasts and many other important subjects. He shared the spirit with us.

Harvesting Chardonnay

Barrels Close the Playground

Whichever wines we create and however we blend them, from various grape varieties, vineyard sources, and fermentation techniques, they are all still wines at the beginning. No sparkle. On the other hand they are not finished table wines. For they are unrefined, high in acid, and somewhat lower in alcohol. In time they will achieve real dimension, but first we will add the bubbles.

The traditional way to produce a champagne style of wine—the one Dom Pérignon perfected—is the *méthode champenoise*. It's also referred to as "fermented in the bottle." Each bottle of traditional champagne is an individual fermenting "container" holding its own wine.

To change still wine to sparkling wine, just before filling the bottles we add a small, precise amount of sugar and a live, active culture of wine yeast. The bottles are then capped, stacked, and the interaction of the yeast and sugar begins. Fermentation of the sugar takes place within each bottle.

This sugar fermentation produces a small increase in alcohol, plus the formation of carbon dioxide gas. And the yeast, as it grows, creates a substantial deposit which—with extended aging—adds great complexity and flavor to the wine. The gas can't escape from the bottle, so it dissolves in the liquid, creating a sparkling wine.

We have created "Stars in the Wine."

from top:
Analysis in the Lab
Measuring Alcohol
Juice Meets Fermenter

It may be difficult to believe, but in 1965 it was almost impossible to purchase Chardonnay grapes in the Napa Valley. As popular as Chardonnay is today, there were almost none of these grapes planted back then. But we had made up our minds to use only the traditional grapes of Champagne: Pinot Noir, Pinot Meunier, and Chardonnay. But we couldn't find any to buy.

Our friend Jerry Draper came forward to help again. "Haven't any Chardonnay I can sell you, but I do have five extra tons of Riesling (also scarce in those days). Maybe you can find some larger winery that would be willing to have you deliver the Riesling to them and give you back the equivalent gallons of Chardonnay wine." It was a hope.

I set out on the road to see Bob Mondavi at Charles Krug Winery. I explained my problem and said, "Bob, if we don't find some Chardonnay we can't start." He thought for a moment and replied, "We'd like to help you. Deliver the Riesling and we'll give you back 500 gallons of Chardonnay wine. And we'll try to make it the lowest alcohol we can." I drove away singing.

It was only a week or so until harvest, so I quickly arranged to buy the Riesling from Jerry Draper and have it delivered to the Krug Winery.

And everything went smoothly. Until! We opened the local paper to read that Bob Mondavi had had a falling out with his brother Peter and left Charles Krug to start his own winery! He wasn't even there anymore.

Back into the truck with faint heart and off to see Peter Mondavi. "Peter, do you know about the arrangement I made with Bob to trade Riesling for Chardonnay wine?" His face was blank. "Never heard of it." My heart went from faint to zero. But despite the bitter breakup between the brothers, Peter then said, "If Bob said we'd do it, we will." And three weeks later I picked up the wine and we were on our way.

Ripe Chardonnay

from left:
Riddling Symbols—A Turn A Day

Aging and Riddling Are Finished—Now to Disgorgement

The Art of the Riddler

Riddling Underway

$\mathcal{W}$e had done it all so carefully, but it wasn't working. The underground cellars dug into our mountain now housed about 3,000 stacked bottles of wine—wine that should be fermenting.

But no gas formed. This was our second tirage (laying down of bottled wine for champagne). As we watched and worried about it, we heard a car outside. Hardly anyone knew yet that Schramsberg was occupied, so the arrival of any visitor was an event. We went out to investigate.

Here was no ordinary visitor. This was André Tchelistcheff, the Dean of American winemakers. His family had left Russia in 1918. He was trained as a winemaker in France and eventually emigrated to the Napa Valley.

His son Dimitri had been advising us and we'd come to know André as a true friend. Now he arrived, smiling as broadly as Bacchus himself.

"How did you know to come by at this moment? We are in big trouble and don't know what to do." This guardian of the spirit answered that he had just been driving by and something had told him to drop in and see how we were doing!

We opened some bottles. He sniffed and held the wine to the light. "Sorry, my friends. The yeast culture is not making it and is not going to.

You simply must dump out all 3,000 bottles, make a new yeast starter, and begin again. I'll explain the ways you may have gone wrong and the ways to prevent going wrong in the future." The spirit was in a challenging mood. We started over.

In the bottle the yeast ferments the sugar in about six months if the temperature of the storage area is correct. However, further aging—up to three years or more—with the yeast in the bottle develops great complexity in fine wines. The yeast grows, forming a sediment in each bottle. And this sediment, as time passes, contributes to the flavor and aroma of the wine. Eventually, however, the sediment must be removed.

The bottles must be turned in racks, bringing the sediment down to the neck (riddling). Pressure from the internal gas then is used to blow that sediment out of the mouth of the bottle (disgorging). These techniques are tricky. We can't just call the Department of Employment and say, "Send us two riddlers and one disgorger."

A riddler with the spirit, Francis Rogers, worked down the Valley at Beaulieu Vineyards. Years earlier he had worked in the champagne business back in Ohio when they still made sparkling wines in the traditional way.

Our first tirage—the 1965 vintage—was 2,000 bottles. Francis drove up every few days and patiently taught us how to turn the bottles. We learned to do them two at a time, in one-eighth and one-quarter turns. Slowly the angle of the bottle was increased so that the yeast moved down into the neck. All went well, and in about six weeks of daily turning we had completed our first tirage.

The person credited with designing the racks and the method of turning the bottles, in the early 1800s, was the Widow Cliquot in Champagne. So now an expert from Ohio taught two refugees from the city something a French lady had invented 150 years earlier. That's how the spirit works.

When the yeast is blown from the bottle the wine is totally "dry." The sugar has been almost totally consumed as the gas is created. At this point there is usually a high level of acid in the wine, so a small dose (dosage) of a specially created syrup is added to balance the crispness.

A big fat cork is then put in place and wired down so the remaining gas can't push it out. Months elapse as the syrup comes into harmony with the wine. Then—or maybe a few years later if you're both curious and patient—you drink the wine that has become champagne.

The grape problem wouldn't go away. We were running all over Northern California trying to find Chardonnay and Pinot Noir; with very little success. We had heard that the Beringer Winery had a small block of Chardonnay growing near Yountville, so I went to see Roy Raymond. I explained our difficulty and that we not only needed to find the grapes but had to pick them early; before Beringer would be harvesting for table wine. "Is there any possibility that you could sell us a few tons and let us pick them ourselves?" Roy looked at me, and although he didn't know us well at all said, "Sure, we'll be glad to help. Come in when you want, pick them yourself and just tell me how much you take!"

Our second trip to Champagne was in 1969. We were at the famous cellars of Krug in Rheims. Henri Krug had just showed us around (the spirit is everywhere), and we were seated in his office. Remi Krug then suggested we have a glass of wine. No one objected. Henri disappeared for a few minutes and returned with an opened, unlabeled bottle. Glasses were filled. Remi asked, "How old do you think the wine is?" (We have learned that this kind of question means we are already in trouble.)

It surely was a mature wine, but the fruit was all there. The structure was firm. It was lovely. We guessed ten years. Remi showed us the cork. It was dated 1928! The wine was over forty years old and still shining.

The Krug brothers explained that the wine had been at the docks awaiting shipment when World War II broke out. Everything was returned to their cellars; labels were removed, and the bottles were stacked away. The Krugs had hoped to avoid seizure of the wine by the occupying German forces. They succeeded, and the wine re-emerged at the end of the war. Now if that isn't coming head on to the spirit, what is?

Grapes on Their Way to the Press

Pinot Noir and Chardonnay in Hand

*I*t was late in the summer, just before the beginning of our third harvest. In order to avoid buying additional fermenting tanks, and in an effort to conserve our limited funds, we had arranged to deliver some of our grapes to the just-opened Sterling Winery and make some of our still wine there. We would then bring the wine back to Schramsberg, make our blends, and produce champagne.

One day a stranger drove into the yard and got out of his car. He showed us his identification as a United States Federal Agent and said that he had heard we were going to make some wine at Sterling this harvest. "If you do that," he said, "you can't label your wine the way you are doing now. You can't say that the champagne was made at Schramsberg." That was not our understanding of the regulations and so we argued with him. But he stood firm. Finally he said, "Well, you can appeal this decision to Washington." We had three weeks to harvest and there was not enough time. It was a potential disaster. There was only one way out. We would have to make all the wine ourselves and not gamble on a timely and favorable ruling from the government. But how? We didn't have the capacity to use all the grapes we had committed to buy.

There is a piece of equipment called a transport tank. These tanks are small and fit in the back of a pickup truck. Winemakers use them to haul small quantities of wine from place to place. We thought—since they are small, the volumes of wine will not overheat, refrigeration wouldn't be required, and maybe they'd work as fermentors. If we could only find a few to borrow!

I got on the phone and began calling everyone I knew. "Would you by chance have a small transport tank we could borrow for the harvest to use as a fermentor? We're in trouble." Before that day was over, four friends had loaded small tanks into their own trucks, driven them to Schramsberg, unloaded them, and put them in place for us to use!

$\mathcal{W}$e had never really been salesmen in our earlier life. Yet someone had to go out and tell people that we had our first 2,000 bottles to offer. A fellow showed up one day and urged us to hire him to sell our wines. We explained that we were going to have to do this task ourselves, since we couldn't afford to hire someone else. "You really don't understand, do you?" he replied. "Nobody thinks you'll be able to make these wines and certainly nobody thinks you'll be able to sell them." He drove off shrouded in another kind of spirit.

But again and again it turned out we were not alone in believing in what we might accomplish.

A printing genius, Jim Beard—along with a dear friend and fine artist, Frank Ashley— helped us design our labels. Our close associate Bob Bonaparte hauled sample bottles around the country while on his own business and made sales. We sought trade leaders and told our story, which was so personal that it elicited interest. Hardly anyone said no, and the 2,000 bottles of champagne were sold. You can understand why we never stopped believing in the spirit.

Davies' First Vintage—1965

Seasons of Dining

The bubbles really set champagne apart from other wines. Romance, congratulations, weddings, New Year's Eve, and much more. (Football players even pour it over each other!) Foaming up the center of a beautiful flute glass there is nothing to equal the visual appeal of a sparkling wine.

In Europe, champagne is also understood to be truly a "wine." With the many styles available it is often enjoyed there as part of a fine dining experience. This has not always been the case in America, where the traditional mind-set has been for "launching brides and boats." Happily that is changing. More and more wine lovers are beginning to understand the complexity, depth, and character possible in a fine sparkling wine and what a wonderful addition it can be to almost any menu.

Think about it. If you choose an elegant variety of grapes such as Chardonnay or Pinot Noir, pick them carefully, bring them from several different vineyard settings, ferment them skillfully (some in barrels and some in tanks), blend the wines in an artistic way, and then age them substantially—why should they not be as suitable an accompaniment to fine cuisine as any excellent table wine? They can be. And that is becoming more widely appreciated. The consumption of premium, bottle-fermented sparkling wines has been growing steadily in America for a number of years.

Bread and Wine

One Month Before Harvest

The role sparkling wines can play in concert with superb cuisine is exciting and fascinating. The various styles and characteristics can complement a wide range of dining. Let us share some memorable moments with you.

Two Kinds of Fermentors

We have been very proud of the many times when Schramsberg has been served at the White House and at other important State events. One of the most memorable occasions, of course, was the evening in Beijing when our Blanc de Blancs was presented at the banquet where President Nixon opened the path to a new relationship with China. The events leading up to this historic moment were amazing. For some time, we didn't appreciate what was really happening.

One day we received a phone call from a gentleman who said he was with the State Department. He explained that they wanted to serve our wine at a dinner in New York. Would we be willing to deliver thirteen cases to the Travis Air Force Base near us, so that same day it could be flown back to the East Coast? "We can't find enough of your wine back here," he said. This was in the days when we produced about 1,000 cases a year! My son Bill and I drove the boxes over to Travis and delivered them personally. We were told to handle the billing through a retailer in Washington.

A few weeks later the phone rang again. This time it was Maxine Cheshire, a journalist with *The Washington Post*. She said: "Tell me how your wine has been selected to be served in Beijing for President Nixon's dinner with the Chinese leaders—in The Great Hall?" I told her I knew nothing about it. She didn't believe me, and urged me to tell her the whole story. I could only say, "If you find out Schramsberg really is going to be served over there, please let me know!" She hung up.

A few days later the phone rang once more. This time it was very early one morning, before we were even up and about. It was our friend at Freemark Abbey winery, Ann Carpy. She said, "Get up, get out of bed, turn on the television set—they are pouring your wine in China!" Of course we jumped. And there it was—right before our eyes. Barbara Walters was holding a bottle on the screen, describing a little-known winery in the Napa Valley, whose wine had been served at this great historic event. That was really a "bright" morning!

Over the years, our experiences with the White House have been both memorable and wonderful. On one occasion we had a call indicating that they wished to serve our wine at the Second Inaugural Luncheon for President Reagan. As you might imagine, we were thrilled.

We were told that there was a proposal to serve our Blanc de Noirs, and the Chef would be

calling us to work out the details. That happened shortly and Jamie talked with him. The Chef explained they were planning to serve our Blanc de Noirs with dessert. What did we think? Jamie explained to him that our Crémant Demi-Sec might be the more logical choice—depending on the dessert. The Chef replied: "Madam, you do not understand. The people in Washington are very sophisticated. They do not care for sweet wines!" Jamie was taken back a bit but responded. "Oh really. You mean the people in Washington do not care for Château Yquem or Barsac? They do not like Trockenbeerenauslese wines?"

There was a long pause. The Chef then responded, "Well, perhaps we should give it a trial run. I'll prepare the dessert and we'll taste your Blanc de Noirs and Crémant with it." He hung up. A week or so later he called back and said, "You were right Madam, it tasted beautifully and Crémant is what we will serve with the dessert."

And to cap it all off, we were invited to attend the luncheon in the rotunda of the Capitol Building in Washington and watched our wine being used to toast President Reagan as he began his second term of office. One more unforgettable moment.

An event we will always remember took place in June 1983 with Chefs Julia Child and Bradley Ogden. It was held in Santa Barbara, California and was one in a series of "Dinner at Julia's." The experience was very personal and a lot of fun.

Bicentennial Blanc de Noir

Dinner at Julia's

Chefs Julia Child & Bradley Ogden
June 1983

Olympia Oysters & Cheese Wafers
SCHRAMSBERG BLANC DE BLANCS 1980

Dungeness Crab Appetizer
Avocado & Pink Grapefruit
SCHRAMSBERG BLANC DE NOIR 1978

Braised Sweetbreads Gourmande
Braised Carrots & Broccoli
SCHRAMSBERG CUVÉE DE PINOT 1980

Chef Brad Ogden's Sugarbush
Maple Mousse & Macaroons
SCHRAMSBERG CRÉMANT DEMI-SEC 1980

Julia's Sweetbreads & Chicken Livers

Serve in ramekins or baked pastry shells.
Yield: 10–12 servings

Ingredients for the Sweetbreads:

1 pound sweetbreads

2 tablespoons butter

¼ cup each; finely diced carrots, celery,
   onions, and boiled ham

4 parsley sprigs, ½ bay leaf, ¼ teaspoon
   thyme tied in washed cheesecloth

½ cup chicken stock

1 ½ cups quartered fresh mushrooms tossed
   in 1 tablespoon fresh lemon juice

Ingredients for the Livers:

2 cups (1 lb.) duck or chicken livers

Salt and pepper

½ lb. flour on a plate

2 tablespoons butter

1 tablespoon cooking oil

2 tablespoons minced shallots or scallions

½ cup chicken stock

⅓ cup dry Port wine

Ingredients for Final Sauce:

1 tablespoon cornstarch blended with

1 cup heavy cream

Drops of lemon juice

3 to 4 tablespoons butter

Preparation of Sweetbreads:

Wash sweetbreads, pulling off loose membranes, and refrigerate in several changes of cold water for several hours, pulling off membranes as they soften. Melt butter in small flameproof baking dish. Stir in diced vegetables and ham. Cover and cook slowly for 10 minutes until vegetables are tender but not browned. Season with salt and pepper. Arrange sweetbreads over vegetables, basting with cooking juices. Add the herb package, cover, and cook slowly for 10 minutes; basting and turning the sweetbreads once. Pour in the chicken broth and enough wine barely to cover the sweetbreads. Cover and cook at the barest simmer, basting several times, for 35 minutes. Blend in the mushrooms and cook ten minutes more. Correct seasoning and let sweetbreads sit in the liquid 30 minutes.

Preparation of Livers:

Pick over the livers to separate the lobes and remove any dark spots, filaments, and fat. Dry in paper towels. Before cooking, season lightly with salt and pepper. Just before sautéing, toss in flour, then toss in a sieve to remove excess flour. Melt the butter and oil in a heavy 10-inch skillet and, when bubbling has almost stopped, add the chicken livers. Stir over high heat for 4 to 5 minutes, until livers have stiffened slightly. Add the minced shallots or scallions, toss for a few seconds, then pour in the stock and wine. Stir and simmer for two minutes more and correct the seasoning to taste.

Final Assembly:

Drain the sweetbreads and vegetables and cut the sweetbreads into pieces about the same size as the livers. Place the sweetbreads and the vegetables in a saucepan; drain the livers and add them to the sweetbreads. Rapidly boil down all cooking juices until reduced by half. Add the cream and boil until sauce is slightly thickened. Pour it over the sweetbreads and livers, taste carefully and correct the seasoning. Shortly before serving bring to the simmer for a moment, remove from heat and swirl in the butter. Spoon into the ramekins or pastry shells and serve at once.

One of the earliest Schramsberg dinners we experienced in Europe was held at The Dorchester in London in 1985. Visualize being in one of the most elegant and historic hotels of England. The food, service, and decor were classic. Here is the menu.

The presentation of two vintages with the main course and dessert, together with the excellence of the cooking made an unforgettable evening for us. The choice of our Cuvée de Pinot (now our Brut Rosé) with the fruit course was marvelous.

Summer Grill and Brut Rosé

*Dinner at
the Dorchester*

London, 1985

❧

Terrine de Homard et Brocoli
BLANC DE BLANCS 1971

Steak de Veau en Croûte
Pommes au Gratin
Légumes du Marché
BLANC DE NOIRS 1977
BLANC DE NOIRS 1979

Trois Mousses de Fruits de la Saison
CUVÉE DE PINOT 1978
CUVÉE DE PINOT 1980

Café
Petits Fours

The Second Epoch

Chef Larry Forgione
An American Place, New York City, 1985

❦

Oysters and Crab Sharing a Shell
Chicken and Chanterelle Brochettes
BLANC DE BLANCS 1982

———

RESERVE 1975

———

Fresh New York State Foie Gras
with Apple & Onion Relish
BLANC DE NOIRS 1975

———

Medallions of Veal & Maine Lobster
with Schramsberg Cuvée de Pinot Sauce
& Baked Virginia Corn Pudding
CUVÉE DE PINOT 1982

———

Salad of Wild Greens & Baby Lettuces

———

Baked Comice Pear
with Pecan Cream & Maple Vanilla Cream
CRÉMANT DEMI-SEC 1982

*I*n 1985 we were celebrating our second decade in the business and were offered the opportunity to present a Schramsberg evening called "The Second Epoch" at the fabled An American Place Restaurant in New York with Chef Larry Forgione. Larry is one of the nicest people you can meet and is wholly committed to excellence. It was a superb menu.

Larry is one of America's truly outstanding Chefs and you will surely enjoy this recipe for a delicious Foie Gras course—for four guests.

Labels Next

Larry Forgione's Foie Gras

Yield: 4 servings

Ingredients:

Flour for dredging

½ cup milk

1 large egg

¼ cup finely chopped blanched almonds

¼ cup finely chopped pecans

¼ cup finely chopped walnuts

¼ cup fresh bread crumbs

Four ½-inch thick slices fresh foie gras
    (about 6 ounces in all)

2 tablespoons olive oil

Salt and freshly ground black pepper

Apple and red onion relish *(recipe follows)*

2 tablespoons finely chopped fresh chives

Preparation :

Spread the flour in a shallow dish. Beat the milk and egg together in another shallow dish. Combine the nuts and bread crumbs in a third shallow dish. Dredge each slice of the foie gras in the flour, dip it in the egg wash and then coat evenly with the bread crumb mixture. Put the foie gras on a baking sheet covered with wax paper.

Heat the olive oil in a large nonstick skillet over medium-high heat. Add the foie gras and cook for 1 minute until golden brown on the bottom. Carefully turn the pieces over and brown on the other side. Drain on paper towels. Spoon the relish into the centers of four serving plates and place the foie gras on top. Sprinkle with chives and serve immediately.

Apple & Red Onion Relish

Ingredients:

1 red onion, diced

1 tablespoon unsalted butter

2 tart apples, peeled, cored, and diced

1 ½ tablespoons red wine vinegar

¾ teaspoon freshly ground black pepper

1 small red bell pepper, cored, seeded,
    and finely diced

3 tablespoons chopped flat-leaf parsley

Preparation:

Put the onions in a strainer and run hot water over them for 2 minutes. Drain well. (This rids them of acidity.) Heat the butter in a large skillet over high heat until it foams. Add the onions and apples and cook, stirring and tossing for 1 to 2 minutes. (Apple pieces should keep their shape and be crisp-tender.) Remove the pan from the heat and stir in the vinegar and pepper. Transfer to a bowl, stir in the bell peppers and parsley and cover to keep warm.

In October of 1985 we were celebrating our 20th Anniversary at Schramsberg. We held a luncheon in our vineyard setting and included friends from all over California. The Chef was the brilliant Jeremiah Tower of "Stars" in San Francisco. Consider this meal!

Here's the recipe for the wonderful Summer Pudding.

Ready to Serve

Anniversary Luncheon

Chef Jeremiah Tower
Schramsberg Vineyard, 1985

❦

Assorted Oysters on the Half Shell
with Sauce Mignonette
Grilled Smoked Duck Brochettes
with Red Onion Confit
BLANC DE BLANCS 1982

⸺✦⸺

RESERVE 1975

⸺✦⸺

Grilled Mixed Seafood Platter
with Drawn Champagne–Lobster Butter
& Tomatillo Salsa
BLANC DE NOIRS 1975

⸺✦⸺

Petaluma Rabbit Stew
with Wild Mushrooms & Fresh Herbs
CUVÉE DE PINOT 1982

⸺✦⸺

Summer Pudding
with a Crémant Champagne Berry Purée
CRÉMANT DEMI-SEC 1982

⸺✦⸺

Assorted Bon Bons & Cookies
Coffee or Tea

Summer Pudding
with a Crémant Champagne Berry Purée

Yield: 6–8 servings

Ingredients:

1 ½ cups strawberries, hulled

1 ½ cups raspberries

1 cup red currants, stemmed

1 cup blueberries, loganberries, or olliberries

1 cup sugar

1 pinch salt

2-3 cups Schramsberg Crémant Demi-Sec

2 cups raspberry purée

10 to 15 slices brioche

2 cups Crémant Crème Anglaise

Preparation:

Pick over and rinse all the berries. Coarsely chop strawberries and put them in a saucepan with the other berries. Add Crémant to cover. Steep the berries for half an hour. Strain off the Crémant. Add sugar and salt and cook over high heat for 5 minutes or until berries are heated and begin to release their color. Remove from heat and cool. Line a 1 to 2 quart pudding mold or other deep bowl with cheesecloth. Dip some of the brioche slices in the berry purée and arrange around the sides and bottom of the bowl. Layer the heated berries with the remaining unsoaked brioche slices. Using a plate that fits just inside the bowl place it on top of the pudding. Put the bowl in a pan. Weight down the plate and refrigerate the pudding overnight. To serve, unmold the pudding onto a serving platter. Slice and serve with the Crémant Crème Anglaise.

Crémant Crème Anglaise

Ingredients:

2 cups whole milk

1 cup vanilla bean, split, or 3 drops vanilla
    extract

5-6 egg yolks

¼ cup sugar

¼ cup Schramsberg Crémant

Preparation:

Scald the milk; if using the vanilla bean, leave to infuse in milk for 10 minutes. Whisk the egg yolks and sugar until thick and light, 3 to 4 minutes. Add Crémant and stir in the hot milk. Return the custard to the pan and heat gently, stirring constantly with a wooden spoon until the custard thickens slightly. Remove the custard from the heat immediately and stir in the vanilla extract. Strain into a very cold bowl. Cover tightly to prevent skin from forming as it cools. Do not overcook or boil custard as it will curdle.

Cruise Dinner

Chef Susan Spicer
Cunard Sea Goddess II, 1991

❖

Shrimp Remoulade
BLANC DE BLANCS 1983

———

Cream of Garlic Soup

———

Grilled Duck Breast with Pepper Jelly Glaze
BLANC DE NOIRS 1984

———

Summer Pudding with Fresh Berries
CRÉMANT DEMI-SEC 1987

*I*n 1991 we had a magnificent invitation to go aboard the Cunard *Sea Goddess II* as wine gurus with the creative Chef Susan Spicer from Bayona, in New Orleans, to orchestrate the food. This was a gala cruise! Our departure was from Stockholm, then we visited Helsinki and St. Petersburg, with Copenhagen as our final port of call.

Here is one of the beautiful dinners Susan arranged with our wines as accompaniment.

Delight your guests with Susan's Grilled Duck Breast for eight people.

Susan's Grilled Duck Breast

Yield: 8 servings

Ingredients:

8 boneless duck breasts (6 oz each).
> You can buy 4 whole ducks, 4 to 5 lbs.—
> and use the legs for roasting or braising.

1 tablespoon coarse salt

1 teaspoon ground pepper

½ teaspoon thyme

½ teaspoon rosemary

Preparation:

Make broth from bones, necks, and giblets, strain and reduce to 1 to 2 cups.

Mix salt, pepper, and herbs and sprinkle on skin side of duck breasts. Refrigerate for several hours or let stand ½ hour before cooking.

Grill breasts over hot coals about 10 to 12 minutes with skin side down, then turn and cook another 3 to 5 minutes. Remove from the heat, let stand 5 minutes, then slice each breast at a slight angle into 5 or 6 pieces and arrange on plate, skin side up.

Hot Pepper Sauce

Ingredients:

4 oz. hot pepper jelly

2 tablespoons chopped shallots

6 oz. sherry vinegar

1 fresh Jalapeno, seeded and finely minced

Preparation:

Combine ingredients in a small sauce pot and cook over medium heat till reduced by half. Add a cup of duck broth and reduce to ½ cup of liquid. Whisk in ¼ pound unsalted butter, a little at a time until sauce is thickened and glossy. Season with salt to taste (pepper shouldn't be necessary) and spoon over the sliced duck breasts.

In 1992 we were ready to introduce our newest sparkling wine, J. Schram. This was such a momentous occasion that we debated seriously about where and how to introduce it. After much thought we decided the best place would be London. We arranged to use an elegant old Mayfair home and invited hundreds of friends from the United Kingdom and the United States, all of whom helped to make this presentation event an evening to remember.

While in London, we also had the opportunity to host an all-Schramsberg dinner at the famed Danesfield House, with the following menu.

This was the first public dinner at which our "new baby" J. Schram was served and it was an unforgettable occasion.

Dinner

Danesfield House, London, 1992

Canapés
BLANC DE BLANCS 1986

—————

Crisp Roast Calves Sweetbreads with Parfait of Foie Gras on Toasted Brioche
CUVÉE DE PINOT 1987

—————

Saddle of Venison with Blueberries, Apples & Chestnuts
BLANC DE NOIRS 1984

—————

Mature Farmhouse Cheeses

Assiette of Desserts
J. SCHRAM 1987

In October of 1992 we introduced J. Schram in America. One of the kick-off events was sponsored by the Breitsteins, of the Duke of Bourbon, San Fernando Valley, and it was held at the Paramount Studios. It was classic Hollywood—Klieg lights, The Buddy Collete Jazz Quartet, and friends from all over Los Angeles. Take a look at what we served.

That night we basked in the limelight like movie stars!

Dinner

Paramount Studios, Hollywood, 1992

*Chicken Satay, Prosciutto con Melone,
Mini Crab Cakes, Smoked Salmon Canapés*
BLANC DE BLANCS 1987

Spinach Tortellini with Pesto and Pine Nuts
CUVÉE DE PINOT 1988

*Seared Tuna Salad with Light Soy/Garlic
Vinaigrette*
BLANC DE NOIRS 1985

*Roast Rack of Lamb with Rosemary and Tamari
Panache of Wild Rice, Grilled Fresh Vegetables*
J. SCHRAM 1987

Cream Bistro-Style Berries
CRÉMANT DEMI-SEC 1988

In March of 1993 we had the unique experience of hosting, in the Napa Valley, a delegation from The Ministry of Agriculture—People's Republic of China. The visit flowed from the fact that we had been to China twice in the past and had met a number of people in the Chinese wine industry; including representatives of the Ministry.

The dinner was held at the elegant Auberge du Soleil. The Chef was David Hale who was in command at that time. Here's the charming presentation:

Dinner

Chef David Hale
Auberge du Soleil, Napa Valley, 1993

Canapés

Duck Prosciutto
Shaved Fennel, Parmesan. Fresh Fruit
RESERVE MAGNUM 1984

Starter

Housemade Lobster Sausage Salad
Asparagus Blood Orange Mustard Vinaigrette
BLANC DE NOIRS 1984 L.D.

Main Course

Roasted California Pheasant
Savoy Cabbage, Portobello Mushrooms
Oregon Huckleberry Sauce
BLANC DE BLANCS 1989

Dessert
Toasted Almond "Cannolis"
CRÉMANT DEMI-SEC 1988

Maine Lobster Sausage Salad

Yield: 18 servings

Sausage Ingredients:

4 pounds lobster meat

2 pounds scallops

½ cup baby carrots (slightly sweated)

½ cup onions (slightly sweated)

½ cup celery (slightly sweated)

3 teaspoons chopped parsley

12 ounces lobster butter

Salt

Cayenne pepper

Hog casings

Preparation of the Lobster Butter:

Preheat oven to 300 degrees. Rinse the lobster shells and roast them for 10 minutes. Pour 1 pound of whole butter over them. Roast for two hours. Cool and begin whipping in cold whole butter with the lobster butter. Continue adding whole butter until the consistency is thickened. Add a bit of tomato paste for color.

To complete the dish:

Mince the vegetables and parsley. With fine blade, grind 2 pounds of the lobster with scallops and the lobster butter. Combine remaining ingredients, season to taste and stuff into the hog casings. Poach the stuffed sausages in simmering water until they reach an internal temperature of 140 degrees. Quickly stop the cooking by immersing the sausages in ice.

Salad Ingredients:

4 shaved fennel bulbs

Pinch of saffron

1 ounce Pernod

1 ounce olive oil

Salad Preparation:

Toss the salad and present with sausage on the side.

Picnic Grounds in the Schramsberg Vineyard

1995 marked our thirtieth year in the wine business and we celebrated from coast to coast with good friends everywhere. We had two ideas in particular to help commemorate in a special way.

The first was to present an unusual cuvée—one with very special character and aging. Earlier we had selected our 1984 Blanc de Noirs and left a thousand cases resting on the yeast deposit for ten years. We now had a special label created marking it as our "30th Anniversary Cuvée." Happily, the world loved it.

The second big thrust of energy was to establish a wine-oriented chef's scholarship at the new Culinary Institute of America school in the Napa Valley, in collaboration with the James Beard

Foundation. We arranged six wonderful fund-raising events with James Beard chefs across the country. The kick-off evening, away from the winery, was in New Orleans with our dear friends the Brennan Family. The dinner was held at Commander's Palace on September 10th, 1995.

The menu speaks for itself.

You'll love this Truffle Risotto recipe from Chef Jamie Shannon.

Jamie and Jack—30th Anniversary Celebration

Dinner

Chef Jamie Shannon
Commander's Palace, New Orleans, 1995

Louisiana choupique caviar with corn & thyme johnny cakes
touched with Creole cream cheese & brunoise of sweet shallots

BLANC DE NOIRS 1984—30th Anniversary Cuvée

Chicory Farm raised whole milk goat & sheep cheese soubise tart
Finished with a sauté of Honey Island Swamp chanterelles
& touched with champagne butter

J. SCHRAM 1989

Southern game bird consommé of pheasant, quail, poussin & mallard duck
accompanied by a panéed foie gras terrine, pink-eyed peas
& Big Daddy's popcorn rice

RESERVE 1987

Point de Chene jumbo lump crabmeat & baby asparagus tips
served with a truffle risotto & complimented by lemon truffle oil

BLANC DE BLANCS 1989

Fig pecan linzertorte with white chocolate chip fig swirl ice cream & port glaze

CRÉMANT DEMI-SEC 1991

Café brulot & assorted pralines

Truffle Risotto

Yield: 4 servings

Ingredients:
3 tablespoons olive oil
1 medium onion, diced
3 cloves of minced garlic
2 cups popcorn rice or arborio rice
1 cup chardonnay wine
3 cups crab stock or seafood or chicken
    stock
2 tablespoons white truffle oil
1 tablespoon sliced truffles
Salt and cracked black pepper to taste

Preparation:
Sauté onions and garlic in a heavy gauge sauce pot with olive oil until onions are clear, add the rice and stir with wooden spoon for two minutes or until coated with oil.

Note: Do not burn garlic and onions and do not let rice stick. Deglaze with the white wine, stir until absorbed. Add half the stock, constantly stirring. When stock is absorbed, gradually add remaining stock while stirring for 15 to 20 minutes. Keep the rice creamy— do not let it stick or become dry. Taste to make sure it is not undercooked, add salt and pepper. Remove from the heat, add truffles and truffle oil. Serve immediately.

Two Products of Nature

In recalling these moments, we can only begin to convey the warmth and goodwill that has been extended to us by our colleagues in the world of cuisine. To adequately express our gratitude for their kindness over the years is almost impossible. This is one Season that surely never ends.

Davies Family in the Olive Lane
John, Hugh, Jamie, Jack, and Bill, with Jessie

pages 110–111:
Vineyards From the Air

Seasons to Come

*W*inemakers are part of something that has been going on between people and the land for a very long time. There is a connection between the vine and enjoyment of life. Winemakers feel they have a hand in something that carries on a tradition of art, of history, of striving; they are true partners with nature. We are fortunate to be among the many current guardians of a spirit that has been alive for centuries. We are doing something other than "getting rid of grapes." And, as that spirit has evolved over the centuries, it will continue to do so in the seasons ahead.

It was in 1986 that we decided the time had come for us to strive for another breakthrough— something really significant for America. We had been the first to do several things with sparkling wines in America but we thought we must go to bat again. We wanted to aim for the very top; to produce a wine that could stand among the finest in the world. We gathered together our young winemakers Alan Tenscher, Mike Reynolds, and Todd Graff. We talked about possibilities, about refinements, about grape sources, and we got down to work. A year later we made the first of these wines, drawing on over fifty lots of base wine and using over fifteen of them in the final blend.

Nature Together

pages 114-115:
March in the Vineyards

The Next Generation

from top, left to right:
Awaiting Judgment
Bottled Art
Winemaker Mike Reynolds

We planned to age this new creation many years before disgorging.

We reached out for Denis Kliene, whom we hadn't seen in years, but who had helped us with our packaging almost twenty years earlier. We worked with him for months searching for something original, artistic, and redolent of history. We reached out to France, where the specialty wine bottle makers are, and began developing the shape of an original and significant bottle.

In 1987 we bottled the first vintage and laid it down for aging. We decided to call it J. Schram in honor of Schramsberg's founder. And it was this wine that we introduced to the world in 1992.

The future for all vintners draws us to seek new vineyards to harvest, new grape varieties to try, new blends to age, new yeast cultures to ferment, new aging cycles, new styles of finish, and on and on. But there is more to this world—there are the people.

The people of Champagne have always been most gracious to us. We can look back to precious moments at Bollinger, Pol Roger, Roederer, Moët-Chandon—to name only a few of the welcoming places. On one of our early trips to Champagne we arranged an introduction to the owners of the famous Roederer Champagne

Magic of the Vine

Bud Break

Sending It to Wine

Cellars in Reims. Jean-Claude Rouzaud and his wife Béatrice invited us for luncheon in their home. We had with us our three young sons aged six, eight, and ten at the time. When we arrived at the Rouzauds' they immediately called out to their own young ones and all the children went off to play. As the afternoon progressed Jean-Claude said, "I've an idea. Why don't we trade children for a summer!" And so our boys spent the first half of the next summer with the Rouzaud family in Champagne, Normandy, and Paris. Their son Stéphane came to Napa for the last half of the summer and again the following year.

Our sons subsequently experienced summer stints with Moët-Hennessy, Rémy Martin, and the Domaine Ott Vineyards in Provence. And they also spent time in Spain, Italy, and Peru. In turn we have had young people from France, Australia, Austria, South Africa, and New Zealand working with us.

Our youngest son Hugh finished his Master's Degree in Viticulture and Enology at The University of California, Davis, in June of 1995. To gain foreign experience he asked for a seasonal job with Moët-Chandon in France, and they welcomed him. He then went to work in the harvest "down under" with Petaluma Winery in Australia. What lies behind these open doors? What keeps them open over the centuries? Hugh is now working with us full-time as our Enologist and preparing for the years ahead.

Our oldest son, Bill, worked for years with other wineries and wine distributors in sales. He later joined us in collaboration with partner wineries in the eastern and southeastern states. He is now with us as Director of Sales. Another road is open.

When we had first set foot on this path in 1965, there were but two other traditional champagne producers in America. We became the third. Within three years we were visited by executives from a very prominent Champagne house. "We see what you are doing here. We are impressed. We'd like to buy your winery!" We told them we treasured our enterprise and would prefer not to sell. "Then we must come to Napa," they replied—and they did.

Today there are dozens of traditional *méthode champenoise* makers in America, including seven of the great names of France and the two premier houses of Spain. The tradition moves onward and upward and across borders and language. And surely the spirit will stretch on into the future; even farther than it reaches into the past. The willingness to share, to help, to learn, to care for nature; to understand and respect people that are unlike ourselves—is all part of it.

Robert Louis Stevenson said it most evocatively when he reflected on his moments at Schramsberg in the 1800s:

> " . . . yet the stirring sunlight, and the growing vines, and the vats and bottles in the cavern, made a pleasant music for the mind.

Here also, earth's cream was being skimmed and garnered—this stir of change and these perpetual echoes of the moving footfall, haunt the land. Men move eternally, still chasing Fortune; and, Fortune found, still wander."

In the fall of 1994 Scottish BBC sent film crews all around the world retracing the steps of Robert Louis Stevenson. They were putting together a film to commemorate the 100th year since Stevenson's death. They came to Schramsberg.

Can you imagine watching an elegant and dapper actor, looking exactly like Stevenson, standing on the veranda of the old Schram home, leaning on the railing and gazing out—as another actor did a voice-over; quoting Stevenson's words, from his book *Silverado Squatters,* describing being at Schramsberg more than 100 years earlier?

The spirit lives on, and we can only be grateful.

pages 124–125:
Upper Vineyard

123

pages 126–127:
A Place to Enjoy the Sun

pages 130–131:
Bountiful Fruit

A Long View Back

1660-70
First sparkling wines made in Italy and England.

1668
Dom Pérignon appointed Chief Cellarer at Hautvilliers.

1673
First underground caves (called "Biscornettes Cellar") dug at Hautvilliers.

1670-1715
Dom Pérignon produces his first sparkling wine using corks.

1775
American Revolution begins.

1826
Jacob Schram born on May 26 in Pfeddersheim on the Rhine River.

1833
Annie Christine Weber born October 2 in Hocheim, Germany.

1838
First vineyards planted in the Napa Valley by George Yount.

1840
Schram arrives in New York. Learns and practices barbering.

1841-42
First grape harvest in the Napa Valley.

1848-49
California Gold Rush begins—bringing thousands of Chinese workers to America.

Basket Wine Press from the 1880s

Jacob and Annie Schram

1853
Jacob Schram starts journey to San Francisco via Isthmus of Panama.

First Napa Valley wine produced by George Yount.

1854
Schram arrives in San Francisco aboard steamer *Yankee Blade*. He opens "Metropolitan Theatre Tonsorial Parlors" in the City.

1856
First sparkling wine made in California by Benjamin Davis Wilson near San Gabriel.

The Barn Cornerstone

1857
First commercial wine shipment from the Napa Valley.

Schram goes to White Sulphur Springs as a barber.

1859
Jacob Schram and Annie Christine Weber are married on February 6.

John Patchet begins first commercial winery in Napa Valley.

1861
Civil War begins in the United States.

1862
Count Agoston Haraszthy returns with 1,400 varieties of grape cuttings from Europe.

Herman Schram born to Jacob and Annie on April 23 in the City of Napa.

The Schrams purchase property on Mount Diamond in Napa Valley and begin development of vineyards and winery. They move onto property August 12.

1865–66
First harvest and crush at Schram's winery.

1867
First successful California sparkling wine from Buena Vista Vinicultural Society.

1869
Completion of transcontinental railroad and release of thousands of Chinese workers.

1870
Schram has planted 30,000 vines; Chinese now digging wine caves for him.

1876
Phylloxera first appears in California but not serious at Schramsberg.

Schram ships 22 cases of his wine to New York.

1879
Schramsberg Winery produces 12,000 gallons of wine. Schram's vineyard now totals 60,000 vines, mostly foreign varietals.

1880
Robert Louis Stevenson visits Schram and later describes Schramsberg in his book *Silverado Squatters*.

August Harvest

1881

Second set of underground cellars begun at Schramsberg and Schram produces 25,000 gallons of wine that year.

1883

Schram plants 20 acres of new vineyard and begins construction of a large barn.

1888

Second set of cellars completed.

1889

Menu from The Palace Hotel, San Francisco, shows Schramsberg and Inglenook as the only California wineries listed.

1891

Schramsberg now producing Zinfandel, Sauvignon Vert, Burgundy, Hock, Sauterne, and Riesling styles of wine.

1905

Jacob Schram dies; property inherited by son Herman.

1914

World War I begins.

1920

Prohibition enacted under the 18th Amendment to the Constitution.

1921

Schramsberg purchased by Captain Raymond C. Naylor as a summer home.

1923

Jack Davies born on June 19 in Cincinnati, Ohio.

1933

Prohibition repealed.

1934

Jamie Peterman born on December 8 in Pasadena, California.

1939

World War II begins.

1940

Schramsberg purchased by John Gargano and his California Champagne Company.

1951

Schramsberg purchased by Douglas Pringle. He revives winemaking for both table wines and champagne.

1957

Schramsberg declared an Historical Landmark by the State of California.

1960

Douglas Pringle dies. Winery closes down.

Jamie Peterman and Jack Davies married in the Memorial Chapel at Stanford University.

Jacob's Olive Lane

Cave Dug by Chinese Workers

1962
Schramsberg awarded membership in The One Hundred Year Club by State of California.

1965
Schramsberg purchased by Jack and Jamie Davies. A renaissance in American *méthode champenoise* begins. They produce America's first BLANC DE BLANCS style of sparkling wine from Chardonnay grapes.

1968
Davies introduce CUVÉE DE GAMAY from the Napa Gamay grape; a rosé style.

1969
U.S. sends Apollo 11 for the first landing on the moon.

Norman H. and Charlotte Strouse create The Silverado Museum in Napa Valley, honoring the 1880 visit of Robert Louis Stevenson.

1971
Schramsberg produces America's first BLANC DE NOIRS style using the red grape Pinot Noir to make a white wine.

1972
Schramsberg produces America's first CRÉMANT style sparkling wine using the Flora grape variety.

Schramsberg BLANC DE BLANCS served by President Nixon in Beijing for Premier Chou En-lai.

1973
First European champagne producers begin establishing wineries in the Napa Valley.

1975
Schramsberg served at White House State Dinner by President Ford for Emperor Hirohito.

1976
Schramsberg served by President Ford at White House Bicentennial Dinner for Queen Elizabeth 11.

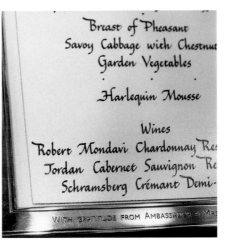

from top:
Royalty at the White House
Schramsberg in London

1977
President Carter serves
Schramsberg at State Dinner
for President Portillo of Mexico.

1978
Diplôme de L' Excellence
Européane, Paris, presented to
Schramsberg.

1979
Schramsberg replaces the style
CUVÉE DE GAMAY with
CUVÉE DE PINOT, using
Pinot Noir grapes.

President Carter's State Dinner
in Vienna serves Schramsberg
for Secretary Brezhnev of the
Soviet Union.

1980
Introduction of Schramsberg
RESERVE—Vintage 1974, aged
on the yeast four years. An
innovation in the American
market.

1983
Schramsberg served at State
Dinner in Williamsburg
for The World Summit of
Industrialized Nations.

1984
California Museum of Science
and Industry in Los Angeles
presents Schramsberg with
Junipero Serra Award for
Excellence.

1985
Schramsberg served at Inaugural
Luncheon for President Reagan.

State Dinner at The White
House with Schramsberg
CUVÉE DE PINOT served for
Prince Charles and Princess
Diana of Great Britain.

Schramsberg purchases the
historic and adjacent M'Eckron
estate; bringing together two
pieces of American wine history.

Smile With the Bubbles

Cook's Magazine presents Jack Davies with Who's Who of Cooking Award.

Schramsberg receives *Wine Spectator* Critic's Choice Award.

1986
Hand-carved Schramsberg Salamanazar created by David Sugar and Carol Iselin and later placed in Liberty Island Museum, New York.

1987
Official banquet with Schramsberg, in San Francisco for Pope John Paul II.

1988
National Geographic Society selects Schramsberg BLANC DE BLANCS to celebrate its 200th Anniversary.

President Reagan serves Schramsberg at White House banquet for Prime Minister Margaret Thatcher.

1989
Schramsberg launches the first American wine venture in Europe: Caves Transmontanas in Portugal.

President Bush serves CRÉMANT DEMI-SEC at dinner honoring the Prime Minister of Pakistan.

1990
Schramsberg served at luncheon for President Mikhail Gorbachev in San Francisco.

1992
Schramsberg introduces its new J. SCHRAM in London.

1993
American Classic Extraordinary Award to J. SCHRAM 1987, San Francisco.

1994
J. SCHRAM served at banquet for Emperor and Empress of Japan; Asian Art Museum, San Francisco.

1994
IWSC, London, awards Gold Medal to J. SCHRAM 1988.

Gardens—A Work in Progress

New World International Wine Competition presents J. SCHRAM "Best New World Wine" Award.

J. SCHRAM also awarded American Airlines "New World Grand Champion" at NWIWC event.

1995
The Davies celebrate 30th year at Schramsberg with series of scholarship fund-raising dinners for the James Beard Foundation and the Culinary Institute of America.

President Clinton serves CRÉMANT DEMI-SEC at White House Banquet for Helmut Kohl, Chancellor of Germany.

Schramsberg served at White House by President and Mrs. Clinton to honor recipients of National Medal of Arts and Charles Frankel Awards.

Bill Davies joins Schramsberg as Director of Sales.

1996
Jamie and Jack Davies presented the Wine and Spirits Professional Award for 1996 by The James Beard Foundation. Schramsberg presented Annual Industry Award by the International Festival of Méthode Champenoise.

Prime Minister of Japan serves Schramsberg BLANC DE BLANCS at luncheon for President and Mrs. Clinton in Tokyo.

Hugh Davies joins the Schramsberg wine-making team as Enologist.

The Way In

Index

Page numbers in *italics* refer to illustrations.